Mastering Transitions

Biblical Principles and
Key Strategies for Advancement

Table of Contents

Message for you

Thank you so much for choosing to be a master in transition. It is an honor and a privilege to join you on this journey as you embark on achieving your purpose. I wanted you to know that I am very proud of you. I am proud of the person you are and your relentless pursuit of improvement. This workbook will add value to your life and provide the tools and strategies necessary for living a purposeful life. Get ready; you are about to embark on a journey of mastering transitions.

Introduction

Life is a series of transitions, each with challenges, opportunities, and lessons. Yet, many people struggle to navigate transitions effectively. Regardless of age, everyone, at some point, has had to deal with a transition. A baby born had to deal with the transition of being out of their mother's womb. A toddler had to deal with the transition from being fed to self-feeding. A teenager must deal with the transition of independence while still being dependent. An adult has to deal with the transition of responsibilities. Everyone deals with a transition. It is inevitable, yet it can be overwhelming. No matter how hard one prepares, one must deal with the transition's side effects. People may feel stuck, overwhelmed, or unprepared for the changes life demands.

I do not write from the perspective of one who has never dealt with transition. I write from the perspective of a man who has had to deal with the transition of losing a mother, moving to a new continent and country, getting married, running a business and a family, and handling everyday challenges that come with being human. After many failed attempts, trauma, and a failed suicide attempt, I had to learn how to expect and adapt to transition, which is why I created this workbook. It is designed to equip you with the tools and mindset to master life's transitions, maximize every season, and move confidently into the future.

Transitions often define the trajectory of our lives. They are moments where decisions shape destinies. By mastering transitions, you'll survive changes and thrive in them. The principles in this workbook stem from two key biblical texts: 2 Timothy 4:6-8 and John 17:1-5. These passages show how Jesus and Paul approached their transition.

Transitions are about moving from one phase to another and maximizing the lessons and opportunities within each phase. Transitions require intentionality, reflection, and action, whether you're transitioning in your personal life, career, or spiritual journey. Drawing from the lives of Jesus and Paul, this workbook offers timeless principles for navigating transitions with purpose and grace.

CHAPTER 1

Biblical Insights
on Transitions

Paul's Example: 2 Timothy 4:6-8

"For I am already being poured out as a drink offering, and the time of my departure is at hand. I have fought the good fight, I have FIN-ISHED the race, I have KEPT the faith. Finally, the crown of righteousness is laid up for me, which the Lord, the righteous Judge, will give to me on that day, and not to me only but also to all who have loved His appearing." NKJV

Paul was giving a farewell discourse as he prepped Timothy on maximizing seasons. He started by saying this to him in 2 Timothy 4:1-5- *"I charge you therefore before God and the Lord Jesus Christ, who will judge the living and the dead at His appearing and His kingdom: Preach the word! Be ready in season and out of season. Convince, rebuke, exhort, with all long-suffering and teaching. For the time will come when they will not endure sound doctrine, but according to their own desires, because they have itching ears, they will heap up for themselves teachers, and they will turn their ears away from the truth and be turned aside to fables. But you be watchful in all things, endure afflictions, do the work of an evangelist, fulfill your ministry."*

Paul then gives Timothy a reason why he can charge him on this by providing Timothy and us a reflection on his life in verses 6-8, saying three groundbreaking sentences.

1. **"I have fought the good fight."**

2. **"I have finished the race"**

3. **"I have kept the faith."**

He says that because of these three things, a crown of righteousness, a reward, and a legacy have been laid up for me. He emphasizes that he expects a reward because he has met the prerequisite for one.

Interestingly enough, Jesus Christ had a similar statement to Paul in His farewell discourse in John 17:1-5:

"Jesus spoke these words, lifted up His eyes to heaven, and said: "Father, the hour has come. Glorify your son, that your son also may glorify you, as you have given Him authority over all flesh, that He should give eternal life to as many as you have given Him. And this is eternal life, that they may know You, the only true God, and Jesus Christ whom you have sent. I have glorified you on earth. I have finished the work which you have given me to do. And now, O Father, glorify me together with yourself, with the glory which I had with you before the world was."

This text is at the climax of Jesus' farewell discourse. He has washed His disciple's feet and informed them of His betrayal and departure and the coming of the Holy Spirit. In Chapter 17, in the closing moments of His life, as the betrayer's plot and plan are in motion, **He prays**, one for Himself, for His disciples, and the world, and in His communication with God, we see similar words utilized to those of Paul the Apostle.

These passages show two great men highly regarded in the Christian faith: Our Savior and Lord Christ Jesus and Paul the Apostle to the Gentiles. **Both men are dealing with the transition of seasons.** Christ gave a farewell discourse as He prepped His disciples for His transition to the Father and the introduction of the Holy Spirit. In contrast, Paul gave a farewell discourse as He prepped Timothy on maximizing seasons.

In His farewell prayer, Jesus reflects on His mission and relationship with the Father. He identifies key accomplishments:

1. **"I have glorified You on earth."**

2. **"I have finished the work which You have given Me to do."**

3. **"Now glorify Me together with Yourself."**

Similarly to Paul, Jesus anticipated the reward of His faithfulness and obedience. Why? What would cause a savior of the world to find Himself, in the closing chapter of His physical season on earth, to utter the words, *"I have finished the work which you have given me to do."* Or what would cause a man whose life and purpose paved the way for the gospels to reach many gentile nations to say in his closing hours, *"I have fought the good fight, I have finished the race and kept the faith."* Two words: **self-assessment.**

These two men demonstrated a key character trait needed for mastering transitions: the ability to self-assess. Based on the effectiveness of their assessment, they concluded that their season was over, and they were ready for the transition. To master transition, you must master self-assessment.

CHAPTER 2

Key Principles for
Mastering Transitions

1. Self-Assessment and Reflection

Both Jesus and Paul demonstrated the importance of self-assessment and reflection. They evaluated their progress and aligned their actions with their purpose.

Merriam-Webster defines self-assessment as *"The process of analyzing and evaluating oneself or one's actions."* While Cambridge University defines it as *"A judgment, sometimes for official purposes, that you make about your abilities, qualities, or actions."*

Self-assessment and self-reflection are key traits of highly self-aware people. According to Travis Bradberry, *author of Emotional Intelligence 2.0, Self-awareness is so critical for job performance that 83% of people with high self-awareness are top performers. Professors at the Education University of Hong Kong studied* the effects of self-assessment on students' academic performance, and the results showed that self-assessment interventions had positive and meaningful effects on students' academic performance.

According to the Academy of Management Perspectives, individuals who assess their progress are likelier to achieve their personal and professional objectives. Self-assessment positively influences self-regulation skills, including goal setting, planning, and monitoring. John Wooden once said, "A mistake is valuable if you do four things with it—**recognize** it, **admit** it, **learn from** it, and **forget** it."

> "Without proper self-evaluation,
> failure is inevitable."

As I asked you earlier, what would cause a savior of the world to find Himself? In the closing chapter of His physical season on earth, he utters, "I have finished the work which you have given me to do." Or what would cause a man whose life and purpose paved the way for the gospels to reach many gentile nations to say in his closing hours, *"I have fought the good fight, I have finished the race and kept the faith."* Two words: **self-assessment.**

> "When you do not do the work
> of self-assessing, you self-repeat."

Here are five common challenges of the effect of no self-assessment:

Biased self-perception

Without self-assessment, we risk overestimating our strengths and downplaying our weaknesses. This bias creates blind spots that hinder growth and success. Recognizing this tendency allows for a more balanced view of ourselves, leading to realistic expectations and better decision-making.

Self-Assessment Prompts

- What are my greatest strengths? Am I overestimating any of them?

_____

_____

_____

_____

_____

_____

_____

_____

_____

_____

_____

_____

_____

_____

_____

_____

_____

_____

_____

_____

_____

- What weaknesses or areas for improvement have I been avoiding?

_____

_____

_____

_____

_____

_____

_____

_____

_____

_____

_____

_____

_____

_____

_____

_____

_____

_____

_____

_____

_____

- How do others perceive me compared to how I perceive myself?

_____

_____

_____

_____

_____

_____

_____

_____

_____

_____

_____

_____

_____

_____

_____

_____

_____

_____

_____

_____

_____

_____

Lack of feedback

Feedback is essential for growth. Without it,
we operate with an incomplete understanding of our performance.
Engaging with constructive feedback provides valuable insights and
helps us align our self-perception with reality.

Self-Assessment Prompts:

- Who can I trust to give me honest feedback?

- What feedback have I received recently, and how have I acted on it?

_____

_____

_____

_____

_____

_____

_____

_____

_____

_____

_____

_____

_____

_____

_____

_____

_____

_____

_____

_____

_____

- In what areas do I need more external input to improve?

_____

_____

_____

_____

_____

_____

_____

_____

_____

_____

_____

_____

_____

_____

_____

_____

_____

_____

_____

_____

_____

_____

_____

Difficulty in self-reflection

Self-reflection requires honesty and intentionality.
Without it, we risk misinterpreting our behaviors and attitudes,
leading to repeated mistakes and stagnation.

Self-Assessment Prompts:

- What recurring patterns do I notice in my actions and decisions?

_____

_____

_____

_____

_____

_____

_____

_____

_____

_____

_____

_____

_____

_____

_____

_____

_____

_____

_____

_____

_____

- How do my behaviors align with my values and goals?

- What lessons have I learned from recent successes or failures?

_____

_____

_____

_____

_____

_____

_____

_____

_____

_____

_____

_____

_____

_____

_____

_____

_____

_____

_____

_____

_____

_____

_____

_____

_____

Emotional bias

With no self-assessment, emotions can cloud judgment and impact self-assessment accuracy. Emotions can cloud judgment and distort our ability to assess situations accurately. Emotional bias leads to impulsive decisions and hinders progress.

Self-Assessment Prompts:

- How do I typically react when I'm stressed or emotional?

_____

_____

_____

_____

_____

_____

_____

_____

_____

_____

_____

_____

_____

_____

_____

_____

_____

_____

_____

_____

_____

- Are my emotions influencing my decisions more than they should?

_____

_____

_____

_____

_____

_____

_____

_____

_____

_____

_____

_____

_____

_____

_____

_____

_____

_____

_____

_____

_____

- What strategies can I use to separate emotions from objective analysis?

_____

_____

_____

_____

_____

_____

_____

_____

_____

_____

_____

_____

_____

_____

_____

_____

_____

_____

_____

_____

_____

_____

_____

Unrealistic goal setting.

Without self-assessment, goals often lack specificity, achievability, and alignment with our true capabilities. Unrealistic goals lead to frustration and decreased motivation.

Self-Assessment Prompts

- Are my current goals realistic and achievable?

_____

_____

_____

_____

_____

_____

_____

_____

_____

_____

_____

_____

_____

_____

_____

_____

_____

_____

_____

_____

_____

_____

_____

- How do my goals align with my skills and resources?

_____

_____

_____

_____

_____

_____

_____

_____

_____

_____

_____

_____

_____

_____

_____

_____

_____

_____

_____

_____

_____

_____

_____

_____

- What smaller steps can I take to make my goals more attainable?

_____

_____

_____

_____

_____

_____

_____

_____

_____

_____

_____

_____

_____

_____

_____

_____

_____

_____

_____

_____

_____

_____

_____

For Jesus and Paul to make these statements, they had to spend time alone reflecting, assessing, and better preparing for their transition.

Reflection Questions:

- How can you address biased self-perception in your life?

_____

_____

_____

_____

_____

_____

_____

_____

_____

_____

_____

_____

_____

_____

_____

_____

_____

_____

_____

_____

_____

_____

- What steps will you take to incorporate feedback into your growth?

- What strategies can you use to overcome emotional bias?

CHAPTER 3

Six Critical Areas
to Reflect On

Spiritual Growth and Progress

• How have I grown spiritually compared to last year?

_____

_____

_____

_____

_____

_____

_____

_____

_____

_____

_____

_____

_____

_____

_____

_____

_____

- How close is my relationship with God right now?

- Am I consistently praying and seeking Him?

_____

_____

_____

_____

_____

_____

_____

_____

_____

_____

_____

_____

_____

_____

_____

_____

_____

_____

_____

_____

_____

_____

- How disciplined am I in fasting?

- Am I committed to studying His Word and applying it?

- What areas of my spiritual life have improved, and what needs work?

_____

_____

_____

_____

_____

_____

_____

_____

_____

_____

_____

_____

_____

_____

_____

_____

_____

_____

_____

_____

_____

_____

- What challenges or strongholds affected me this year?

_____
_____
_____
_____
_____
_____
_____
_____
_____
_____
_____
_____
_____
_____
_____
_____
_____
_____
_____
_____
_____
_____
_____
_____
_____

- What spiritual goals should I set for the new year?

- What habits or influences should I nurture or remove?

_____

_____

_____

_____

_____

_____

_____

_____

_____

_____

_____

_____

_____

_____

_____

_____

_____

_____

_____

_____

_____

_____

Goal Setting:

- Write one spiritual goal for this year:

_____

_____

_____

_____

_____

_____

_____

_____

_____

_____

_____

_____

_____

_____

_____

_____

_____

_____

_____

_____

_____

_____

- **Steps to achieve it:** 1.

_____

_____

_____

_____

_____

_____

_____

_____

_____

_____

_____

_____

_____

_____

_____

_____

_____

_____

_____

_____

_____

_____

- **Steps to achieve it:** 2.

- **Steps to achieve it:** 3.

_____

_____

_____

_____

_____

_____

_____

_____

_____

_____

_____

_____

_____

_____

_____

_____

_____

_____

_____

_____

_____

_____

_____

Mental Growth and Transformation

- Have I grown mentally, or do I still think the same way?

_____

_____

_____

_____

_____

_____

_____

_____

_____

_____

_____

_____

_____

_____

_____

_____

_____

_____

_____

_____

_____

- How has my focus improved or changed this year?

- What consumed most of my attention this year?

- Did I create and stick to a plan for last year?

_____

_____

_____

_____

_____

_____

_____

_____

_____

_____

_____

_____

_____

_____

_____

_____

_____

_____

_____

_____

_____

_____

_____

- What obstacles kept me from achieving my goals?

_____

_____

_____

_____

_____

_____

_____

_____

_____

_____

_____

_____

_____

_____

_____

_____

_____

_____

_____

_____

_____

_____

- What specific plans should I create for this year?

_____

_____

_____

_____

_____

_____

_____

_____

_____

_____

_____

_____

_____

_____

_____

_____

_____

_____

_____

_____

_____

_____

_____

- Who must I become to reach my next level of growth?

_____

_____

_____

_____

_____

_____

_____

_____

_____

_____

_____

_____

_____

_____

_____

_____

_____

_____

_____

_____

_____

_____

_____

- What actions, books, or mentors will help me?

_____

_____

_____

_____

_____

_____

_____

_____

_____

_____

_____

_____

_____

_____

_____

_____

_____

_____

_____

_____

_____

_____

Goal Setting:

- Write one mental growth goal for this year:

_____

_____

_____

_____

_____

_____

_____

_____

_____

_____

_____

_____

_____

_____

_____

_____

_____

_____

_____

_____

_____

_____

_____

- **Steps to achieve it:** 1.

_____

_____

_____

_____

_____

_____

_____

_____

_____

_____

_____

_____

_____

_____

_____

_____

_____

_____

_____

_____

_____

_____

_____

_____

_____

_____

- **Steps to achieve it:** 2.

- **Steps to achieve it:** 3.

_____

_____

_____

_____

_____

_____

_____

_____

_____

_____

_____

_____

_____

_____

_____

_____

_____

_____

_____

_____

_____

_____

Health and Fitness

- Am I healthier this year compared to last year?

_____

_____

_____

_____

_____

_____

_____

_____

_____

_____

_____

_____

_____

_____

_____

_____

_____

_____

_____

_____

_____

- How well have I cared for my body?

_____

_____

_____

_____

_____

_____

_____

_____

_____

_____

_____

_____

_____

_____

_____

_____

_____

_____

_____

_____

- Where did I fall short in maintaining a healthy lifestyle?

- What foods or habits negatively affected my health?

_____

_____

_____

_____

_____

_____

_____

_____

_____

_____

_____

_____

_____

_____

_____

_____

_____

_____

_____

_____

_____

_____

- Did I meet last year's health goals?

_____
_____
_____
_____
_____
_____
_____
_____
_____
_____
_____
_____
_____
_____
_____
_____
_____
_____
_____
_____
_____
_____
_____

- What health improvements do I need to prioritize this year?

_____

_____

_____

_____

_____

_____

_____

_____

_____

_____

_____

_____

_____

_____

_____

_____

_____

_____

_____

_____

_____

_____

_____

_____

_____

- What habits, diets, or routines will support my goals?

Goal Setting:

- Write one health and fitness goal for this year:

_____

_____

_____

_____

_____

_____

_____

_____

_____

_____

_____

_____

_____

_____

_____

_____

_____

_____

_____

_____

_____

- **Steps to achieve it: 1.**

_____

_____

_____

_____

_____

_____

_____

_____

_____

_____

_____

_____

_____

_____

_____

_____

_____

_____

_____

_____

_____

_____

_____

- **Steps to achieve it:** 2.

- **Steps to achieve it:** 3.

_____

_____

_____

_____

_____

_____

_____

_____

_____

_____

_____

_____

_____

_____

_____

_____

_____

_____

_____

_____

_____

_____

_____

Finances

Section Finances into Spending
| Earning | Savings | Investments | Giving

- How am I managing my finances? Break it down into spending, earning, saving, investing, and giving.

_____

_____

_____

_____

_____

_____

_____

_____

_____

_____

_____

_____

_____

_____

_____

_____

_____

_____

- Am I spending more than I earn?

_____

_____

_____

_____

_____

_____

_____

_____

_____

_____

_____

_____

_____

_____

_____

_____

_____

_____

_____

_____

_____

_____

_____

_____

- Am I saving or investing wisely?

_____

_____

_____

_____

_____

_____

_____

_____

_____

_____

_____

_____

_____

_____

_____

_____

_____

_____

_____

_____

_____

_____

- Did I faithfully tithe or give?

- What were last year's financial goals, and did I achieve them?

_____

_____

_____

_____

_____

_____

_____

_____

_____

_____

_____

_____

_____

_____

_____

_____

_____

_____

_____

_____

_____

_____

_____

- What adjustments should I make for this year to improve my financial situation?

_____
_____
_____
_____
_____
_____
_____
_____
_____
_____
_____
_____
_____
_____
_____
_____
_____
_____
_____
_____
_____
_____

Goal Setting:

- Write one financial goal for this year:

_____

_____

_____

_____

_____

_____

_____

_____

_____

_____

_____

_____

_____

_____

_____

_____

_____

_____

_____

_____

_____

- **Steps to achieve it:** 1.

_____

_____

_____

_____

- **Steps to achieve it:** 2.

- **Steps to achieve it:** 3.

_____

_____

_____

_____

_____

_____

_____

_____

_____

_____

_____

_____

_____

_____

_____

_____

_____

_____

_____

_____

_____

_____

_____

Purpose & Destiny

- Am I using my time wisely, balancing moments of action (Kairos) with daily routines (Chronos)?

Chronos - Quantitative - seconds, minutes, hours, days - time that governs our life.

Kairos - Qualitative time - measured by moments, an opportune time for ACTION.

Kairos can also be defined as "Deep time," a time when one can move forward in the present without being tethered to a clock or calendar.

_____

_____

_____

_____

_____

_____

_____

_____

_____

_____

_____

_____

_____

_____

_____

_____

- Where do I stand in the season of my life (learning, doing, or giving back)?

_____

_____

_____

_____

_____

_____

_____

_____

_____

_____

_____

_____

_____

_____

_____

_____

_____

_____

_____

_____

- Am I pursuing my purpose and calling?

- If my life ended today, would I feel fulfilled?

_____

_____

_____

_____

_____

_____

_____

_____

_____

_____

_____

_____

_____

_____

_____

_____

_____

_____

_____

_____

_____

_____

_____

_____

- What steps will help me live more purposefully this year?

- What habits, people, or resources should I align with?

_____

_____

_____

_____

_____

_____

_____

_____

_____

_____

_____

_____

_____

_____

_____

_____

_____

_____

_____

_____

_____

Goal Setting:

- Write one purpose and destiny goal for this year:

_____

_____

_____

_____

_____

_____

_____

_____

_____

_____

_____

_____

_____

_____

_____

_____

_____

_____

_____

_____

_____

- **Steps to achieve it: 1.**

_____

_____

_____

_____

_____

_____

_____

_____

_____

_____

_____

_____

_____

_____

_____

_____

_____

_____

_____

_____

_____

_____

_____

- **Steps to achieve it:** 2.

_____
_____
_____
_____
_____
_____
_____
_____
_____
_____
_____
_____
_____
_____
_____
_____
_____
_____
_____
_____
_____
_____
_____
_____

- **Steps to achieve it:** 3.

_____

_____

_____

_____

_____

_____

_____

_____

_____

_____

_____

_____

_____

_____

_____

_____

_____

_____

_____

_____

_____

_____

Relationships

- Who are the key people in my life (friends, mentors, mentees)?

- Are my relationships helping me grow, and am I adding value to others?

_____

_____

_____

_____

_____

_____

_____

_____

_____

_____

_____

_____

_____

_____

_____

_____

_____

_____

_____

_____

_____

_____

- Are my conversations productive and meaningful?

_____

_____

_____

_____

_____

_____

_____

_____

_____

_____

_____

_____

_____

_____

_____

_____

_____

_____

_____

_____

_____

_____

- Do I surround myself with people who inspire and challenge me?

_____

_____

_____

_____

_____

_____

_____

_____

_____

_____

_____

_____

_____

_____

_____

_____

_____

_____

_____

_____

_____

- Who can I pour into or learn from in the coming year?

_____

_____

_____

_____

_____

_____

_____

_____

_____

_____

_____

_____

_____

_____

_____

_____

_____

_____

_____

_____

Goal Setting:

- Write one relationship goal for this year:

_____

_____

_____

_____

_____

_____

_____

_____

_____

_____

_____

_____

_____

_____

_____

_____

_____

_____

_____

_____

_____

_____

- **Steps to achieve it:** 1.

- **Steps to achieve it:** 2.

- **Steps to achieve it:** 3.

_____

_____

_____

_____

_____

_____

_____

_____

_____

_____

_____

_____

_____

_____

_____

_____

_____

_____

_____

_____

_____

_____

_____

_____

CHAPTER 4

THE MINDSET NEEDED
FOR TRANSITION:

Transitions require a shift in mindset. Romans 12:1-2 says, *"I beseech you therefore, brethren, by the mercies of God, that you present your bodies a living sacrifice, holy, acceptable to God, which is your reasonable service. And do not be conformed to this world, but be transformed by the renewing of your mind, that you may prove what is that good and acceptable and perfect will of God. "*NKJV

Transformation begins in the mind. You can only grow to the height of your thinking. Your natural elevation requires mental elevation. For your life to change, your mind must first change. The average person possesses four levels of mentality. These levels accelerate or hinder the average progression in any individual's life. The four levels are progressional and accessible to anyone open to change. Level 4 is a high-achieving faculty, but few ascend to that level.

Level 1 mentality – "I WILL"

There are those with an "I will" mentality. These are individuals who treat everything in life as an option. Their life's purpose and dreams are an option for them. They approach success, tasks, goals, dreams, and initiatives with an "I will" attitude and mentality. They haphazardly do everything. They operate solely on convenience. As long as things are convenient for them, they will engage in any tasks, but when things get complicated, they quit, walk away, and refuse any form of strain. They will engage in any activity, regardless of the repercussions involved; they are unguarded, careless, and irresponsible. These are low achievers; they never accomplish anything beyond their arm's length. They never reach further for anything because their mindset only operates on convenience. It takes consistent pressure and persuasion to get them to evolve to a level 2 mentality, only to operate out of feeling forced or coerced into being purposeful.

Level 2 mentality – "I HAVE TO"

There are those with an "I have to" mentality. They are slightly better than those with an "I will" mentality but are not elite in their thinking. They approach success, tasks, goals, dreams, and initiatives with strain. They make it seem like everything is inconvenient, and they are pressured to perform. They don't want anything for themselves; they only must be persuaded by people or life circumstances to be productive. Success is an inconvenience for them. Purposeful living is inconvenient for them, and they only work because they have yet to find an alternative. The danger of an individual with an "I have to" mentality is that they will easily forgo a task if a less strenuous opportunity with equal reward presents itself. They are always on the lookout for the easiest way out. When unguarded and with a refusal to grow and evolve, regardless of the dangers associated with choosing an easy way out, they eventually end up falling back into a level 1 mentality individual, choosing any way that produces less stress and more reward.

Level 3 mentality – "I GET TO"

There are those who have crossed beyond the border of vicarious living and carelessness. They approach success, tasks, goals, dreams, and initiatives with gratitude and passion. They have a strong feeling of excitement or enthusiasm for what they do and are driven to pursue it with energy and dedication. They are meticulous in their endeavors and make an effort to see the accomplishment of their goals, but they have one problem – They are solely led by passion, and unfortunately, passion, like anything, can die. When burnout occurs, doubt sets in, and their mindset declines to an "I have to" one. These people have passion, but their passion is not fueled by purpose. Their "I get to" mindset is only effective as long as there is excitement and convenience. As long as everything aligns with their personal agenda, goals, and initiatives, they have an "I get to" mindset, but when it stops being fun. The pressures of purpose set it, they easily succumb to feeling forced to live a purposeful life, and they begin to approach tasks, goals, dreams, and initiatives with an "I have to" effort. Passion without purpose is an opportunity waiting to die. Although they are level 3, for them to achieve ultimate success, they must evolve to a level 4 mentality.

Level 4 mentality – "I MUST"

These are the elite thinkers of society. They approach success, tasks, goals, dreams, and initiatives with an "I must make an effort" mentality. They are not solely led by passion but by purpose. Those with an "I Must" mentality do not operate out of feelings and emotions. They treat life with soberness and seriousness. Each task is a do-or-die thing for them. They do not need pleasure to achieve success. They move with an unstoppable force solely focused on achieving its goal. They are not easily distracted and thrive exclusively on finishing their task. Their goals, dreams, visions, and initiatives come first before any pleasure. Pain does not hinder them because they function based on purpose. They will forgo the inconvenience for a greater purpose. They are not easily distracted, and their purpose consistently regenerates passion for them to get the job done.

The only way to achieve any form of essence in life is to have an "I MUST" mindset and approach to everything you do. It cannot be solely related to a specific task you enjoy doing. You must train your mind to give maximum effort in every task, even day-to-day activities. What you practice in your daily routine, you become in your future. You must first become in your mind what you hope to become in your life.

Reflection Questions:

- Which mindset level (Level 1 to Level 4) do I currently operate in most areas of my life, and why?

_____

_____

_____

_____

_____

_____

_____

_____

_____

_____

_____

_____

_____

_____

_____

_____

_____

_____

_____

_____

- What areas of my life do I treat as optional, and how can I start taking them more seriously?

_____

_____

_____

_____

_____

_____

_____

_____

_____

_____

_____

_____

_____

_____

_____

_____

_____

_____

_____

_____

_____

_____

_____

- When faced with challenges or discomfort, do I tend to quit, find easier alternatives, or push through?

_____

_____

_____

_____

_____

_____

_____

_____

_____

_____

_____

_____

_____

_____

_____

_____

_____

_____

_____

_____

_____

_____

_____

_____

- Are there areas where I rely too heavily on passion without anchoring my efforts in purpose?

_____

_____

_____

_____

_____

_____

_____

_____

_____

_____

_____

_____

_____

_____

_____

_____

_____

_____

_____

_____

_____

_____

_____

_____

_____

- What is one task, goal, or responsibility I need to approach with an "I Must" mindset starting today?

_____

_____

_____

_____

_____

_____

_____

_____

_____

_____

_____

_____

_____

_____

_____

_____

_____

_____

_____

_____

_____

_____

_____

- How do I usually respond when burnout or doubt sets in, and how can I stay focused on my purpose?

_____

_____

_____

_____

_____

_____

_____

_____

_____

_____

_____

_____

_____

_____

_____

_____

_____

_____

_____

_____

_____

_____

_____

- What small, consistent habits can I practice daily to confidently train my mind to approach all tasks?

- Have I ever compromised my long-term goals by choosing convenience over purpose, and how can I avoid this?

- In what ways can I reframe moments of pain or discomfort as opportunities to grow closer to my purpose?

_____

_____

_____

_____

_____

_____

_____

_____

_____

_____

_____

_____

_____

_____

_____

_____

_____

_____

_____

_____

_____

_____

- If I fully embraced an "I Must" mindset, what would my life look like in five years, and what actions can I take today to achieve that?

_____

_____

_____

_____

_____

_____

_____

_____

_____

_____

_____

_____

_____

_____

_____

_____

_____

_____

_____

_____

_____

_____

_____

- What areas of your life require an "I must" mindset?

_____

_____

_____

_____

_____

_____

_____

_____

_____

_____

_____

_____

_____

_____

_____

_____

_____

_____

_____

_____

_____

_____

- What excuses or distractions are holding you back?

_____

_____

_____

_____

_____

_____

_____

_____

_____

_____

_____

_____

_____

_____

_____

_____

_____

_____

_____

_____

_____

_____

_____

Notes:

Write your reflections here...

Conclusion

Mastering transitions is about reaching the next destination and becoming who you need to be to thrive in every season. By following the principles of self-assessment, adopting the right mindset, and prioritizing God's purpose, you can navigate transitions with confidence and clarity. Let this workbook guide you as you step into the next season with faith, focus, and intentionality.

Final Reflection:

- What is your biggest takeaway from this workbook?

_____

_____

_____

_____

_____

_____

_____

_____

_____

_____

_____

_____

_____

_____

_____

_____

_____

_____

_____

_____

_____

_____

_____

_____

_____

_____

_____

_____

- How will you apply these principles in your life?

_____

_____

_____

_____

_____

_____

_____

_____

_____

_____

_____

_____

_____

_____

_____

_____

_____

_____

_____

_____

_____

_____

_____

_____

Notes:

Write your closing thoughts here...

_____

_____

_____

_____

_____

_____

_____

_____

_____

_____

_____

_____

_____

_____

_____

_____

_____

_____

_____

_____

_____

_____

_____

References

1. Merriam-Webster Definition

Merriam-Webster. (n.d.). *Self-assessment*. In Merriam-Webster.com dictionary. Retrieved from https://www.merriam-webster.com

Cambridge Definition

Cambridge University Press. (n.d.). *Self-assessment*. In Cambridge Dictionary. Retrieved from https://dictionary.cambridge.org.

Bradberry, T., & Greaves, J. (09). *Emotional intelligence 2.0*. TalentSmart.

Study on Academic Performance (Education University of Hong Kong)

Academy of Management Perspectives. (n.d.). Self-assessment and goal achievement. Retrieved from https://aom.org

Wooden, J. (2005). *Wooden on leadership: How to create a winning organization*. McGraw-Hill Education

www.ingramcontent.com/pod-product-compliance
Lightning Source LLC
Chambersburg PA
CBHW051523120626
46551CB00012B/1051